WRACK

¶ Of this Edition of *Wrack* one thousand and fifty copies have been printed

Of these nine hundred and seventy five copies only are for sale *240*

WRACK

A Play in Six Scenes

by

PEADAR O'DONNELL

JONATHAN CAPE
30 BEDFORD SQUARE LONDON

FIRST PUBLISHED 1933

JONATHAN CAPE LTD.   30 BEDFORD SQUARE, LONDON
AND 91 WELLINGTON STREET WEST, TORONTO

PRINTED IN GREAT BRITAIN IN THE CITY OF OXFORD
AT THE ALDEN PRESS
PAPER MADE BY GROSVENOR CHATER & CO., LTD.
BOUND BY A. W. BAIN & CO., LTD.

WRACK

CHARACTERS

HUGHIE BOYLE, *and his wife,*
BRIGID BOYLE, *a young couple in the thirties*
MARY JIM, *a neighbour woman about Brigid's age*
KITTY CORMAC, *and her husband,*
PADDY CORMAC, *an elderly couple*
FANNY BRIAN, *an old woman,*
JOHNNY ANTHON ⎫
⎬ *two old fishermen*
CORNEY ⎭
.Other men.

The play takes place during a November evening and night. All the scenes, except the fifth, are in Brigid and Hughie's cottage on an island off the coast of Donegal; the fifth scene is in Johnny Anthon's boat out in the fishing grounds.

SCENE I

The kitchen of a fisherman's cottage, towards evening. The door opens and two women enter. They are returning from a carrigeen moss strand and are wearing sacking as aprons over dark skirts. They have dark neck shawls tied round their heads and are wearing men's boots. They are in the thirties. One is tallish and black-haired, she is BRIGID *the woman of the house. The other is* MARY JIM, *a neighbour woman, fair-haired and less vigorous. She goes eagerly towards the fire, her hands out to the blaze.*

MARY JIM   A good fire is a grand thing: I'm terribly cold this day somehow.

BRIGID (*untying her bag apron and letting it drop off in the middle of the floor*) I'll make us a slug of something hot; it'll be hot anyway. Let the kettle down a link and it will be boiling in a minute.

WRACK

MARY JIM Isn't it grand to have such a fine fire. (*She adjusts the kettle to the flames*)

BRIGID (*kicking off her boots, she is without stockings*) I have Sally's youngsters to thank for it; I'd be lost only for them. There's not a grain of sugar in the house but the drink will warm us.

MARY JIM A body runs out of sugar now and then. (*She yawns*)

BRIGID (*approaching the fire with the teapot from the dresser*) Ah, hold your tongue: I near forget what sugar tastes like in tea. I don't see that it can be any different with you, Mary Jim.

MARY JIM You have the bare tongue of your people, Brigid; it's getting barer.

BRIGID It would need it: devil such a bit of hiding and juking as goes on in this Island. (*Pours water into the teapot to rinse it out*) You'd think we had a member of parliament in every house, we have such lashing and lavings if it's true for us. I be mad with all that pretending. (*She goes down the floor and empties teapot into bucket at the foot of the table*)

MARY JIM And is it crying you'd have us? We'd get a lot for crying.

BRIGID Crying? (*She walks quickly to the fire, leaves the teapot on the hearth, and reaches to the mantelpiece for the tea caddy*) Thank God nobody belonging to me carried their bladders behind their eyes. (*Opens the tea caddy*) Tears is a poor complaint but silly letting on is as poor. (*Flings tea into the teapot and wets the tea*)

MARY JIM It's little some of us knows about the worries of others.

BRIGID More shame for us then.

MARY JIM You should be happy here, Brigid, with your house all to yourself; a second woman on a floor is a trial betimes.

13

BRIGID I'm happy, thank God, but that doesn't keep my guts from roaring with the hunger now and then.

MARY JIM I'd lie down stone dead, Brigid Hughie, if I thought people knew that the house was empty; a wee bit of pretending is all that's in anybody these times. God save us mind your tongue; you never know who might hear you.

BRIGID (*goes to dresser for bowls*) The world is free to hear me then. I'm shutting the door on nobody, and I'll take my Bible oath this minute we're the only house on this island with a weak family that keeps the door open at meal time. Do you? (*Sets bowls on the table and approaches the fire for the teapot*)

MARY JIM Brigid, you're going in the head.

BRIGID (*lifts up the teapot quickly and goes across to the table to pour out the tea*) And did you ever notice the way we be spluttering and coughing getting near one another's door; giving warning we're coming like boats in a fog.

MARY JIM The legs would go from under me if somebody came in on us and us at a meal.

BRIGID God put the queer legs under you then: ah, you sicken me and the rest is like you. Here, drink this (*Hands her bowl of tea*)

MARY JIM And do you think, Brigid, things is the same way with us all?

BRIGID There's not what would salt a herrin' in the differ between the best off and the worst off of us young women. Look-at, I'll go round telling one of you or the other till I make you all so you can't hide.

MARY JIM I'm afraid of you and I run to you; I always ran to you. I used to forge my sums off you at school. But it's easy for you to do as you please with your house all to yourself. Nabla and me is

getting on one another's nerves. We be silent and I
be near choking.

BRIGID If it's not silence it's a spill of talk, and the
silence is the same as the talk; a cover to hide one
mind from the other. Is there a house on the island
with two women on the floor but there's tightness
and sharpness and silence? Is there a houseful of
childer but they're nagging and scratching at one
another? Isn't the whole island in the fidgets? And
what is at the root of it all? I'll tell you, it's hunger;
aye, it is, hunger.

MARY JIM Virgin Mother this day! Brigid, that's
wild talk.

BRIGID (*sets down her bowl on the table and approaches
Mary Jim*) Listen to me, Mary Jim: if you come
with me to the carrigeen strand another day and
carry on the way you done this day, I'll brain you.
Not a word out of you except every now and then a
wheeze of a tune as if something was dying in you:
I used to rasp my fingers on the edges of the rocks

to keep from screeching: what in God's name is wrong with you? Is anything wrong at home?

MARY JIM (*she slumps forward in her seat*) Wee Susan is all caught in her breathing. Nabla said she should be wrapped in black wool sprinkled with gin. Where under God am I to get black wool and gin?

BRIGID I can give you black wool and a sprinkle of gin: It's true for Nabla that'll loosen any cold.

MARY JIM Amn't I the useless woman, Brigid, that never has things like the rest of you!

BRIGID I'm rich because I have a pick of wool and a spoonful of gin (*She goes back to the table and rests against it*) I wish to the good God that the herrin' would come.

MARY JIM I'm not able to hope for anything: I just pull away. I'm that lazy now I don't want to get up. I'll be that lazy when I go home I won't want to get out of my wet clothes. Did you ever notice how sleepy you get when you sit at the fire in your wet clothes? I hate to change.

BRIGID I hate the slapping of wet skirts on my legs. I hate all this pulling and driving and mean living; it's making me a kind of risen. And there's more like me. Look at the way we're wearing out: it's only the other day you were a fly-a-way butter-fly, and now, look at you. Still let the herrin' come and we'll all be ourselves again. Thank God I have the heart to be fond of life no matter what.

MARY JIM I near forget what my heart used to be like; I'm as dead as the sea out there: we might as well be tied together, me and the sea. What life can people have on an island when the life goes out of the sea? And isn't that sea out there dead?

BRIGID Let a cargo of herrin' come in down there and you'll see the life that is in it and the life that's in yourself.

MARY JIM There won't be an herrin' any more.

The sea around this island is dead, I tell you. I saw that when things began to go bad with us.

BRIGID The sea may be empty, but it's not dead; it's IT that's not dead. I couldn't live away from it, I think, bad and all as things are.

MARY JIM (*gets to her feet and faces* BRIGID) I'll tell you the truth what's on me, it's the sea. Am I going queer, Brigid? (*Vehemently*) I hate the sea. I hate to look at it. I hate walk in it. I turn my stomach if I taste it. I would as soon look for milk out of the rotten udder of the dead cow the dogs are tearing at in Point, as go down to the sea these days for anything. If it was living couldn't it give us some share of life? What have we to get as it is? Carrigeen, sloak, dilsk; everything that's dead and clammy.

BRIGID If bad feeling got up between me and the sea, I wouldn't know how to live. Not but I be mad with it when Hughie comes in out of it beat to the world, if he'd only give in. But, Mary Jim, don't

you mind when the herrin' used to be out there?
God send the herrin'.

MARY JIM (*stares into* BRIGID's *face, turns away and
shakes her head*) Nothing could waken me now;
I got worn out. Maybe, if I was somewhere
where I couldn't see the sea . . . everytime I look
at us plucking at the edge of it, I want to leap and up
and tell us all it's dead. I could cry. That's what
makes me sing, I suppose.

BRIGID (*gently*) I'm going up with you, Mary Jim.
You're going to your bed this minute with a hot
pot-lid to your feet. Nabla and me will fix Susan.

MARY JIM (*disengaging herself from* BRIGID's *arm*)
Leave me be, can't you. (*Walks to the door, looks out,
shivers, turns to* BRIGID) While I see that—if I could
only run and run till there was no sea. (*Despairingly*)
I'm late for that. (*Turns to the door again, goes out*)

(BRIGID *hastily snatches a shawl off the kitchen
line and flings it on her shoulders. Goes quickly
to the door, looks left and then right, obviously*

*sees something that holds her eye. She clears
her throat and calls 'Kitty'. Comes back in,
lifts the sack apron off the floor, hangs it on a
nail on the back door, picks up* MARY JIM'S *bowl
from the hearth, puts it into her own on the table.
An elderly woman, lithe, grey-haired, comes in.
Dressed in coloured blouse, with check apron
over grey skirt. She has a dark neck shawl
tied round her head.* BRIGID *is at the door as*
KITTY *enters.*)

BRIGID Are you in a hurry home, Kitty?

KITTY There's nothing running away on me:
what trot is on you?

BRIGID 'Tis, I'm going up to see Mary Jim's
Susan and I would like to spread my carrigeen. Sit
there, for maybe, Sally's youngsters would take my
childer home before I'm back. I be frightened if
they're in by themselves.

KITTY Seo, well; Nabla was telling me about
Susan. (*Goes up towards the fire*)

WRACK

BRIGID (*pausing outside the doorstep*) I see Fanny Brian coming up from the Caslagh; she'll be company for you.

> (BRIGID *goes off.* KITTY *takes a stool and sets it in the corner facing the audience. Takes knitting needles and yarn from under cover of her apron and rests them in her lap. Takes neck shawl from her head and settles it on her shoulders. Takes out snuff-box and taps lid gently.* FANNY BRIAN, *elderly, dark, gaunt woman in black comes in quickly. Her eyes flash on* KITTY *then search the kitchen sharply and rest on the room door behind* KITTY.)

KITTY There's nobody here but me, Fanny. Were you looking for one of them?

FANNY BRIAN (*obviously excited*) I want to see Hughie. Peter Dan's big boat is out on the ride. (*Walks up and stands rigid near* KITTY)

KITTY Indeed is she; the slip-slap, clitter-clatter of the tide around her bows took a start out of me when I came round the Point. It strikes you all of a sudden. Take a pinch, Fanny. (*Offers snuff-box*)

FANNY (*ignoring snuff-box*) Peter Dan expects herrin'. Before the first streak of dawn the other morning I saw lanthorn light spilling out of the open door of his barn. He was mending a net.

KITTY (*withdrawing snuff-box*) And, under God, what had you up at that hour? It's not sick your cow is again?

FANNY (*more excited*) And this day I watched him for an hour and him stiff against a rock, his two eyes stuck in the sea-gulls in the Bay. And now he has his big boat out. He's going out this night.

KITTY And what's wrong with him going out this night more than any other? It's no bad temper is on the weather this day, Fanny Brian.

FANNY BRIAN Did you see the cobwebs on the grass yesterday morning? Did you see the cormorants on the rocks with their wings out this day? And

23

is there a bird in the whole Bay out there this minute? (*Gestures towards the door*)

KITTY Cobwebs on the grass is rain. Cormorants is birds I never heard heed put in.

FANNY BRIAN (*angrily*) The signs I saw I know the meaning in. And as I was missing the birds out of the Bay I come round the Point and there's Peter Dan's boat on the ride.

KITTY You came on Peter Dan's boat all of a sudden in the dusk. The slapping of the water round her bows took a start out of you. The sea can take a start out of you no matter how well you know it, and us old people be easy to frighten; we be afraid for our men.

FANNY And there on the rock above his boat I saw Peter Dan by himself, and his teeth bare and him looking up at the sky, and the sky with a grig on it glowering back. (*Walks quickly to the door.* KITTY *gets to her feet and follows her.* FANNY *turns to face*

24

KITTY) And the sea is down there now gurning and spitting among the rocks.

(KITTY *goes to the doorstep, thrusts her head out listening.* FANNY *passes out, and again faces* KITTY.)

KITTY That's only the clatter of the claban in the Caslagh at the flood; I always think that's friendly, somehow. Your heart is in your ears, Fanny, and it frightened; it's not the sea you hear at all. Come up and sit. (*Gestures with her head towards the fire*) Us old women is company for one another.

FANNY BRIAN (*gesture of impatience*) There is venom burning and biting in every lip on every wave. I must see Hughie Boyle. (*Looks around wildly*) Where's Hughie Boyle? (*Goes off*)

(KITTY *goes out on the street and looks after* FANNY BRIAN.)

CURTAIN

SCENE II

Same as Scene I: half an hour later. KITTY *has tongs in hand fixing the fire. A man approaches whistling. Comes in quickly, stepping lightly, halts inside the door and looks around. He is tallish, in dark jersey. He is* HUGHIE, BRIGID'S *husband.*

KITTY It's me is before you Hughie.

HUGHIE And where is this woman of mine?

KITTY She must be soon in: she ran up to Mary Jim: Like enough she'll go round to Sally's for the childer. Show me where the things is and I'll make your tea.

HUGHIE (*decisively*) Not at all, Kitty, not at all. I just ran in to say I wouldn't be in for my tea until late. Peter Dan's boarding nets.

KITTY (*gravely*) You're going out the night?

HUGHIE It's a venture we're making, just a venture.

KITTY And does Peter Dan think there is a good appearance on the evening? Isn't the sea restless somehow?

HUGHIE As true as God you'd think the women of this island had the sea in their clothes and that their bodies were raw with it. I'm hearing talk I never heard. I'll lock up that woman of mine from you all or you'll spoil her on me. I'd rather, be heavens, have the tooth-ache than have anybody around me snapping at the sea. Isn't it wonderful you never hear the men at it.'

KITTY It's ease to me to see you angry, Hughie. I wasn't giving in to it myself. Did you see our Paddy at all?

HUGHIE Paddy! The noise of your Paddy is all

over the island. Johnny Anthon's sheep broke in and ate his young cabbage. He thinks it's his own sheep.

KITTY Why the devil couldn't Johnny Anthon's people mind their sheep; not that Paddy will give out much to Johnny. Many a time I tried to put them at it.

HUGHIE Paddy is in a rage. I saw him racing about on his heels like a seaplane. It's you Paddy is blaming.

KITTY I'll hide if he's in a rage like that; don't tell him I'm here.

HUGHIE (*going out*) Didn't I see you out there at the stack for turf, Paddy would be sure to eye you. (*From the door*) What did I tell you, here he comes across the garden (*He grins back at her*) I hope he skelps you. (*Goes out*)

(KITTY *hastily throws a coil of yarn on the back of a chair and begins winding. Her husband,*

29

PADDY CORMAC, *comes in — a lithe, active root of a man in a black jersey, obviously angry. He halts inside the door.*)

PADDY Haumph! (*He shuts the door sharply*) Fine it suits you to be out helping the neighbours to mind their business; you're a grand hand at your own.

KITTY Is it begrudge me to Brigid Hughie for an hour to mind the house for her you'd do?

PADDY (*comes close up to* KITTY) It's not; and fine you know it's not. And damn fine you know it's not. It's my plants; my fine garden of young cabbage.

KITTY (*looking very subdued, takes up skein of yarn and holds it out to him. He hesitates, glances at her angrily but stretches out his arms. She puts the skein of yarn on them and begins winding*) The plants, indeed, aye. (*Sharply*) Well, you'll just have to forget all about them. Don't make an old fair day of it.

PADDY Now, look-at, Kitty, look-at here . . .

WRACK

KITTY As well as that there's not that much harm done, maybe.

PADDY Now, look-at, look-at, stop it Kitty. (*His hands come together as though to fling the thread to her. She waits with an air of exaggerated patience. He resumes holding the thread*)

KITTY (*with a pluck at the skein*) Such a clitter-clatter: And I wouldn't give you a spit for all the harm's done, not a spit.

PADDY Now, look-at, look-at: here, to hell with it.

(*He flings the skein of yarn in on her arm and stamps angrily up to the fire; lifts coal in the tongs and sets it to his pipe and pulls loudly; flings down the tongs with a bang on the hearth. KITTY re-arranges thread on the back of the chair and goes on winding. She steals a look at PADDY but as he wheels round her face grows severe. An elderly man passes the window.*)

KITTY Making an old fair day of it; now, shut your mouth.

(*Before* PADDY *can answer* JOHNNY ANTHON *enters. He too is elderly, but fresher and heavier than* PADDY. *He is distressed and speaks promptly.*)

JOHNNY Too bad about your plants, Paddy, too bad about your plants.

PADDY (*with angry glance at* KITTY) You said it, Johnny Anthon, too bad, too bad.

JOHNNY I was never as put about over anything; they were a purty good ridge of·plants.

PADDY Purty good; is it purty good? Only this morning I was saying to myself that I never saw such a healthy green on anything growing. (*Turns angrily to* KITTY) Oh, look-at, look-at.

JOHNNY (*slightly embarrassed*) Ellen says they were worth every penny of five shillings.

KITTY I wouldn't give you three shillings for them.

PADDY (*loudly, in a rage*) Kitty, now, look-at here, Kitty . . .

(*There is a short silence.* KITTY *goes on winding.* PADDY *turns to* JOHNNY, *continues angrily.*)

Five shillings, Ellen says five shillings. Ellen says —oh, another Kitty, Ellen.

JOHNNY (*hurt and a bit angry*) Well, Paddy Cormac this is the way things is: Five shillings is the best we can do. I'm sorry and Ellen is sorry and there's your five shillings.

PADDY (*sits down suddenly on a chair and stares at* JOHNNY. KITTY *ceases winding and looks on*) What are you blathering about, Johnny Anthon. It's my own sheep that ate the plants. It's Kitty there I'm mad at.

c   33

JOHNNY No, Paddy Cormac, no: fair is fair. It was our sheep. Catch your money.

(JOHNNY *attempts to put the money into* PADDY'S *hand.* PADDY *starts to his feet upsetting the chair.*)

PADDY Nonsense, Johnny Anthon, nonsense. (*Glares at* KITTY *who is again busy.* JOHNNY'S *hand comes towards him again with the money*) I'll be vexed I tell you. (*Turns towards the fire*) Maybe, there's not that much harm done. You never can tell with soft plants.

JOHNNY There's harm done, Paddy Cormac. Well, I'll tell you what; make it what Kitty says, three shillings.

PADDY The less I hear about Kitty . . .

KITTY Doesn't that beat all, me thinking it was our sheep; me blaming myself all the time.

34

(PADDY *snorts*.)

JOHNNY Fine you knew, Kitty, fine you knew.

PADDY (*turning quickly*) I don't want another word about it now from either of you. Don't make an old fair day of it. Don't make another Kitty of yourself, Johnny Anthon. Not one word more.

JOHNNY (*puts the money back in his pocket*) That's a thing I be steadying Paddy Cormac, Kitty often takes a rise out of you. (*Takes up the yarn to hold it for* KITTY) You're hasty, Paddy. You're like Corney in that. I often be steadying to myself lately Paddy, that Corney is the strangest man in the world. Do you ever be steadying about Corney, Paddy?

PADDY (*genially, sitting down*) Corney is set in his notions, I give in to that.

JOHNNY (*sawing the air energetically*) I was saying going home to the two of us last night, that I'll swear I have the worst run of cards put past me this winter

that was ever known on this island. But would Corney give in to me? He would not.

PADDY You're getting a bad run of cards, Johnny,
sure enough; not a worse ever I saw. It would rise
any man.

JOHNNY You said it, Paddy. But I'm going to
have the thing put one way or another this night.
(*A man passes the window*) Wait, here's Corney;
I want Corney to hear this.

(CORNEY, *an elderly fisherman with a slight
stoop enters carrying an unlighted lanthorn. He
too, is in black jersey.*)

JOHNNY Now, Corney, you never agree with me,
but listen all the same. Now, Paddy, my nerves
won't stand any more of yon. I don't mind the bad
cards. I could carry the bad cards, but I can't stand
Andy Mor with his nose on my shoulder every night
and him breathing into my ear. No man could stand
it. My nerves is gone; every hand worse than the

other and Andy Mor's nose going Hooh, hooh at me ear. It'll have to stop or I'll do something I'll be vexed for.

CORNEY Well, God Almighty, if a man can't breathe near you . . .

JOHNNY Now, Paddy, it's to you I'm talking. I'm not talking to Corney; Corney never agrees with me.

PADDY It's no bad wish, Andy Mor has for you then, Johnny.

JOHNNY Don't I know it's no bad wish he has for me, and it's no harm I'm wishing him, but I can't stand yon hooh-hooh into me ear and carry the rubbish of the pack at the same time. I got up on my backside in the bed last night out of a half-sleep, thinking I heard him on the pillow beside me. My nerves won't stand another night of it.

KITTY Why don't you get in under the lamp, Johnny?

JOHNNY (*eagerly*) Kitty, you took the words out of my mouth. Paddy, I'm going in under the lamp in your house this night. (*Darts a challenging look at* CORNEY) That's all that's to it. Kitty agrees with me.

CORNEY Ah, bedamn Paddy, he couldn't do that. You might as well tell me dacently sit at home as to root me out from under the lamp. Doesn't everybody know I can't tell the differ between a heart and a diamond without I'm under that double burner of Kitty's. Ach, Johnny never will be content until he puts the whole world upside down.

JOHNNY Well, I don't want to do something I'll be sorry for, and I will if Andy Mor comes hooh-hooh into my ear this night. I tried a plug of wool last night — not a bit of use; worse.

CORNEY If Johnny was to sit at the foot of the table, Johnny, Andy Mor wouldn't follow him for not a out of the fire would he take his backside to follow anybody. Yon moleskins of his must be as stubborn as pot-metal when they don't go on fire.

JOHNNY (*in despair*) I can't sit at the foot of the table, the cold would get me in the legs. There wouldn't be a bit of understanding between my knees and my toes in half an hour. Isn't that queer now and me never cold about the body? It's just the legs that goes back on me. Maybe, it's the same way with Corney's eyes; they eyes goes back on Corney.

CORNEY They do, they do: I'll see a buoy out there in the bay farther than anybody, but bring a thing close up, especially colours, and my eyes goes clean stupid; there's not the same health in things, somehow, lately.

JOHNNY It runs through my own head often, and I be steadying on it, that if we could only get Hughie Boyle here to ask Peter Dan to let us in we could have many a night in peace. Andy Mor wouldn't have the same race in his feet to Peter Dan's he has to Paddy's.

CORNEY It's only Hughie Boyle here could do it, for nobody else on this island could make freedom of that kind with Peter Dan.

PADDY Hughie Boyle? That man puts heed in nothing only fishing gear and whistling; himself and Peter Dan's well met.

JOHNNY I often be steadying on them two men, they're a strange sight. Two men always together, one of them all the time whistling and the other all the time chewing tobacco; it's as strange a thing as I see on this island.

CORNEY The man that wouldn't listen to Hughie Boyle whistling would be a strange sight.

JOHNNY That's the differ between Corney and me Paddy; nothing ever puzzles Corney. Many's the time I be steadying things that Corney puts no heed in at all.

CORNEY If I put heed in all the wonders Johnny

sees Paddy, I'd be coming round and round, round and round. It's just natural for Peter Dan to listen to Hughie Boyle, that's all's in it.

JOHNNY A man must have a strange nature to be as silent always as Peter Dan; the more I steady on that man the more I be puzzled. Doesn't he puzzle you, Paddy?

PADDY He does, he does. Ah, now you must give in, Corney, yon's strange, never talking.

CORNEY You're as bad as himself, Paddy Cormac. Peter Dan's the plainest man to see in the whole world. Where is there his equal on a helm? Isn't he as at home in the sea as a wave? Isn't he as obliging a neighbour as you'd get in a day's walking? Call him late, call him early, there he is. And Johnny makes a wonder out of a man like that. And you agree with Johnny just to please him, Paddy Cormac. Come on to your cards. I saw Andy Mor putting in a butt of a stack; ten to one he'll be at home threshing.

41

JOHNNY Well, maybe in God. (*Walks towards the door*) Where's Hughie here, Kitty, do you know?

KITTY He's down with Peter Dan boarding nets.

ALL THREE What!

KITTY He said it was just a blind venture they were making.

PADDY Well, under God, if that woman is not a trial. Did you send word to our boys? Under heaven this night — are you daft, woman? Out with us.

(CORNEY *hurries to light his lanthorn*; JOHNNY *and* PADDY *are in the doorway*, JOHNNY *slightly outside.*)

JOHNNY I see light in your barn Corney. Them's good boys of yours Corney. My barn is in darkness. Where's them rascals of mine? Tumbling the house all week because there's nothing to fish, and now

when the fish is here . . . no, no, bedamn, yon
is a lanthorn running up our barn steps; them's
bully youngsters of ours. Look at the racing of the
lights round your gable Paddy Cormac . . . the
youngsters is bully men.

PADDY Is it in my own eyes it is or is that a light
out there near the Black Rocks?

JOHNNY That's Fanny Brian taking the near way
over here, her Charlie is to be fishing with Peter
Dan and Hughie here this season.

PADDY Yon's lights making for the shore from
my barn. My boys is running to the boats with the
nets. I'm away.

KITTY And I'm off too: I had enough of Fanny
Brian for one night. Brigid must be soon in anyway.
(*Goes out after* PADDY, *tying on her neck shawl as she
goes*)

CORNEY Damn this lanthorn it won't light.

WRACK

JOHNNY Out with us Corney; I don't want to begin by meeting a woman on the way to the boat for the first night. It's not dark at all, Corney. Hurry, man alive. I don't want to meet a woman. Anyway, it's not dark. Come on Corney.

(CORNEY *flings a burning match on the floor in disgust, shuts down the lanthorn and goes out with* JOHNNY.)

CURTAIN

SCENE III

Interior of Hughie Boyle's cottage, as before. BRIGID *is sitting on a low stool in front of the fire. She is drying her hair, which hangs in a cloud around her face. The door is open. As she combs her hair she hears* HUGHIE, *her husband, in the distance whistling 'The Road to the Isles'. She hums softly and her voice rises as he comes closer. She ceases abruptly and flings back her hair from her face as he comes to the door. He enters jauntily, oil-coat across his arm.*

BRIGID The devil's in you, Hughie, what kept you, and me with boxty for you? It's spoiled now. Wet tea for yourself. When I got a minute I washed my hair. (*She swings the crane so that the kettle comes into the blaze, her hair tumbles down again over her face.* HUGHIE *hangs up his oilskins*) I suppose the old men trapped you to play cards: you're a bit foolish

45

the way you let yourself be led this way or that by
Johnny or Corney. (*She speaks buried in her hair,*
HUGHIE *looking at her in surprise*)

HUGHIE Who had you in with you?

BRIGID It is then, there never was a night with
such little traffic. The school teacher sat there with
me and I had Fanny Brian in and out twice. (*Her
voice grows troubled*) I had a notion Fanny wasn't
at her ease because the master was in: you had to
drag words out of her. I was, somehow, feeling a
bit down and she made me worse. I thought you'd
never come in. Funny, how a body's heart can be
down and then shoot up.

HUGHIE Didn't you hear the calling down at the
Caslagh?

BRIGID I heard laughing; what was it?

HUGHIE We were boarding nets down at the cliff.
(BRIGID *shakes the hair from her face; she is excited*)

46

BRIGID Boarding nets? You mean there is word about herrin'?

HUGHIE Peter Dan says we are going out as soon as the tide turns to let us down the Narrows.

BRIGID (*leaping to her feet begins fussing about making the tea.* HUGHIE *amused sits at the head of the table*) Well, honest to God, Hughie, the heart will leap through my clothes: herrin'. The devil's in you why didn't you send me word?

HUGHIE Most like we'll have a night out for nothing.

BRIGID Would Peter Dan rush out like this under the eyes of the whole island if the Bay was without fish? For two pins I'd give hunder a burst and cut the bread we have for the morning.

HUGHIE Honest to God, Brigid, we're going on nothing but the carry-on of a few birds. Don't I know? It's ten to one we'll have our night for

47

nothing. (*A pause*) What was wrong with Fanny Brian?

BRIGID Don't be turning my mind back on Fanny Brian. (*After a pause*) She was silent with her neck shawl out over her head: she made me uneasy: I think she's a bit queer. (*She sits down again to dry her hair.* HUGHIE *pours out the tea*)

HUGHIE Once we went to board nets everybody went to board: Corney and Johnny, and Paddy were in their oilskins in a jiffy. And the noise of them, like a lot of childer. (*He puts a slice of boxty on a plate and drops it on her lap. He hands her a bowl of tea*)

BRIGID You were as lucky to be late or there would be noise here: Cormac fell asleep in the corner there waiting for you to bring him the sail you promised.

HUGHIE I cut it for him too: it's on top of a lobster pot up in Peter Dan's barn: wait till he gets yon sail on his wee boat . . .

WRACK

BRIGID Do you ever wonder, Hughie, that it's a pity, maybe, to fill childers' minds with the sea too much? That passes through my mind now and then when I'm down. It's a cogglesome life. Lately, somehow — oh, I don't know.

HUGHIE Don't you get an edge on you against the sea, Brigid, for God's sake. Isn't the sea the most natural thing in the world? You never see that right till you go to a ravelled-up place like a city. Woman dear, the sea is plain to the world.

BRIGID It can be grudging: and it can be sudden.

HUGHIE I wouldn't mind it being sudden if it would stop starving us.

BRIGID Maybe in God you'll get a haul the night. What kind of humour is the weather in? There's no two words in it, Hughie, a body has to keep in mind that the sea can be sudden.

HUGHIE So can a horse, or if it goes to that a man or a woman: even a child that's sickening for the coming of a tooth be's cranky and short. Why wouldn't the sea be fidgety when it's in a tremble with the storm that's coming? But it would be a queer island man that couldn't tell when the sea would be like that.

BRIGID I suppose island childer had best turn their face to the sea.

HUGHIE It's a boat-builder I want Cormac to be. (*He takes a drink of the tea*) When I was wee I used to tell myself that I would be a boat-builder: I was to build boats for all the islands. After every storm I'd be round gathering pieces of sticks for my big boat. And every nail I saw I nabbed it: I had a big canister of nails in a skelpy. Man alive, I'd stand for hours gaping at a new piece of timber and wondering would I ever be able to buy the like. The boat I was to build NO sea could toss.

    (BRIGID *jerks her hair from her face and looks at him.*)

Funny, I don't think that thought was in my mind now these years. Passing the Scotch drifters the day brought it back: Man alive, yon's a great singer on the 'Highland Mary'.

BRIGID It's not easy in your mind you are when you think so much of building big boats.

HUGHIE I be mad at the way things are. Bigger boats would be part of what we want.

BRIGID Funny, what goes on inside people's minds when the sea is worrying them. Nights when you're out and the sky gets mixed, and the bar begins roaring, I have to make myself sit down till I talk to myself. I say to myself, that there's maybe, a hundred boats out along the whole coast and that Peter Dan's crew is the greatest crew of them all. And I tell myself that the most any storm done was to trap one or at most two boats. And then I see the work the waves would have smothering one boat after the other before ever they got the length of putting fight on you. I put myself at ease that way. I pray; it's me does pray, but, it's not the praying that keeps my mind settled but the thinking. I be afraid of the sea sometimes, Hughie. It's great you're such a powerful crew.

HUGHIE Peter Dan's the greatest helmsman between the Foreland and the mouth of the Shannon. He's as natural to the sea as its own waves.

BRIGID Hughie, if the sea ever gets the length of a fight with you, you'll fight as men never fought, won't you, Hughie?

HUGHIE Every man with Peter Dan would be like ten men. But what kind of talk is this?

(*He gets up and lights his pipe.* BRIGID *is running her fingers through her hair.*)

BRIGID You saying that will be fine for a body's mind some night when there's darkness and blasts and a big noise in the sea. (HUGHIE *is cutting tobacco into his fist: he pauses, looking at her*) I be afraid of storms and I like them. Isn't that queer? It's a grand thing to be a woman when your man comes in frozen stiff out of a hailstorm, or, maybe, torn with rowing till every sinew and muscle is on fire. It's then it's a grand thing to be a woman, I'm telling you. (HUGHIE *teases the tobacco in his hand*) I'll never forget the night you staggered coming out of the boat that brought the priest and doctor to Mary Jim, and you put your weight on me coming up the Brae in the hurricane and the sea making murder against the rocks. (*She flings back her hair with a wild gesture*) There's a lot of nature in the world, my boyo.

        HUGHIE *leaves pipe, tobacco and knife on the table quickly and walks over to her.*)

HUGHIE Cormac'd miss a lot if we make a boat-builder of him so. (*He puts a hand under her chin and tilts up her face. A woman's cough is heard outside.* HUGHIE *steps back quickly and picks up his pipe, etc.*)

BRIGID (*in a low voice, coiling her hair*) This is Fanny Brian back: and if there was one night when I'd give a bargain in you, Fanny, it's this minute. (HUGHIE *sits on chair again and proceeds with filling his pipe.* FANNY *comes in with a hurri-*

53

*cane lanthorn in her hand: she sets it down on
the floor.*)
Come up, Fanny, take that creepy, and take out
your stocking, it's early yet. (FANNY *sits down: she
takes out her knitting and rests it in her lap.* BRIGID
looks at her knitting) Aren't you the bully Fanny,
to be able to knit diamond tops. All the colours must
be a bother.

FANNY (*sharply, turning to* HUGHIE) The night got
a lot darker and there's a whistle in the wind that
could be snow.

HUGHIE (*quietly*) There was snow on the moun-
tains this morning.

BRIGID Wouldn't it be grand if we got a spell of
frost to keep the sea calm if the herrin's coming.

FANNY (*still to* HUGHIE) I don't want our Charlie
fishing with Peter Dan.

HUGHIE (*pausing with a lighted match in his fingers*)
You're not the one mind with Charlie on that: he's

a foot higher since he was took on (*He lights his pipe*)

FANNY I won't have our Charlie fishing with Peter Dan.

HUGHIE (*after a puff*) Charlie asked for the place and he got it: maybe, you can make him let go, even his mind is set on it. But I would say take care of what you're doing. If you break his grip on Peter Dan's boat, look out that he doesn't let go his grip on the island, and then where would you be? Wouldn't the whole island laugh at a man that drew back for a woman's talk? (*Puts pipe back in his mouth and smokes*)

FANNY If you put against him Peter Dan wouldn't take him.

HUGHIE And what for would I put against Charlie's good luck?

FANNY (*getting to her feet*) I'll go down on my knees to you, Hughie Boyle, to stop Charlie from fishing with Peter Dan.

55

BRIGID (*coming quickly to* HUGHIE'S *side*) Jesus, Mary and Joseph, Fanny Brian, I'm scared: isn't Hughie fishing with Peter Dan? Hughie I'm scared.

HUGHIE (*who is standing, arm round* BRIGID'S *shoulders*) Choking to you, Fanny Brian: I know what's on you: afraid he'll marry Nellie Ruadh if he makes money. You're all alike, all you old women with sons.

FANNY You don't know what you're saying, Hughie Boyle: I tell you I don't want him fishing with Peter Dan.

(BRIGID *moans.*)

HUGHIE Here, Brigid, away you go till I have this out with Fanny.

BRIGID I don't want to go: I don't want to stay: I never felt this way. I think I'm getting weak. (*Both go towards door*)

HUGHIE Out you go my girl: go down to Sally. (*In a whisper*) she's crazy.

56

(BRIGID *searches his face: he nods assurance:*
she goes out. HUGHIE *shuts door, and walks up*
and faces FANNY.)

Now, Fanny, I'm angry with you. You shouldn't
say things to Brigid that could come back into her
mind at night time when she's alone here with
sleeping childer, and us on the sea, and it rough.
I'm angry with you, Fanny Brian.

FANNY But, under God, can't I make you see?
I don't want our Charlie to be fishing with Peter
Dan.

HUGHIE You're giving myself the creeps. What's
inside your mind at all (*He searches her face with his*
eyes) I'll speak to Charlie. (FANNY *makes a gesture*
of despair; she sits down)

FANNY If Charlie thought I got him off Peter
Dan's boat he'd leave me. Haven't I trouble holding
him as it is: and where is there for him to go: and
I couldn't stand it to see him go out into the hunger

that's in the world for the poor, and to go angry with me too.

HUGHIE What's on you, Fanny? Is it a dread ?

FANNY It's a dread, Hughie Boyle. (*Turns to stare into fire*) A dread. (*She sways to and fro*)

HUGHIE It's foolishness: it'a an old woman's foolishness, Fanny. It's just foolishness. (*He takes a step nearer*) Like a good woman, you'll not talk of this dread with Brigid listening. I want you to promise me that.

FANNY Not a word will be out of me any more. I couldn't keep it down. It's out now. I'll promise you, Hughie Boyle. (*There's a whistle outside*)

HUGHIE That's Peter Dan. I must run down to the Caslagh. Sit there till Brigid comes in and try to be cheery before her. You'll promise me?

FANNY I'm sorry about Brigid. Do you think it's foolishness? (*Swings round and faces him*)

HUGHIE Just foolishness. (*He goes quickly out*)

> FANNY *sits in the corner, the glow of the fire is on her face, her body sways. After a minute the half-shut door comes in with a bang.* FANNY *jumps to her feet and stands rigidly with arms folded across her chest.* BRIGID *comes in and shuts the door behind her.*)

BRIGID (*attempting a lightness*) The wind's on the door now, it's fair from the nor'ard.

FANNY Was it the wind? I'm glad it was the wind. (*Sharply*) The wind went round against the sun.

BRIGID Is there harm in that and it not at the turn of the tide?

FANNY (*agitatedly*) Did you notice the moon, Brigid? Is the moon clear?

BRIGID (*facing* FANNY, *obviously nervous*) I took a good look at the moon: it is by itself and the sky

around it has the colour of ice; there's no trouble
on the moon.

FANNY (*relaxing*) That's good, Brigid, no trouble
on the moon; that's good. (*The two women face each
other in silence*) Put no heed in an old woman,
Brigid; old women be foolish; we be foolish. (*She
sways to and fro.* BRIGID *puts her arms around her*)

BRIGID Are you sick, Fanny Brian?

FANNY (*wildly*) I promised Hughie I would say
no word, but my heart is sunk in blackness and I'm
chiking. (*She loosens the neck shawl round her neck.*
BRIGID *helps her to a seat and kneels beside her*)

BRIGID Mother of God this night, Fanny, tell me.

FANNY (*in a low voice*) Amn't I the bad woman
and me after promising Hughie I would speak no
word that would trouble your mind, Brigid; but
my own mind is roasting in my body.

BRIGID I have no mind, Fanny, nor life, nor
nothing, but Hughie.

FANNY Brigid, if you went down on your two knees to Hughie he'd leave Peter Dan's boat and take Charlie with him. Look-at, I'm down on my two knees to you to go on your knees to Hughie.

> (*They are both on their knees. After a pause* BRIGID *jerks to her feet and staggers to the table; she goes unsteadily to the door, opens it and looks out. Down below in the Caslagh there is laughter and voices.*)

BRIGID The sky is there for the world to see and the sea is broad with the moon on it. Fanny, where, under God, could harm be hid, and the sea that quiet?

FANNY There's harm hid.

BRIGID And all that laughin' down in the Caslagh? (*She wheels quickly and faces* FANNY BRIAN) If I kept Hughie home by some trick and the other men put to sea in their boats, and came back in the morning all scales, roaring to one another, and everybody laughing, could I look Hughie in the face? In his own mind he would be shamed before the island. You're wrong, Fanny Brian; look at the sea; and the shore full of voices. Come to the door here, Fanny Brian. (*Rushes to* FANNY *and hurries her to the door*) Listen to the laughing: listen to the kind of laughing it is. Can't you be like that Fanny Brian. I want to be like that. (*Turns quickly to get a shawl*) I'm going down to the boats. You're going down to the boats: the whole island will be round the boats in the Caslagh and there will be heart in everybody. (*Takes* FANNY'S *arm*) Come on Fanny. (*She gestures towards the door*)

FANNY BRIAN (*turning away from the door*) I think I'll sit here a wee while.

(BRIGID *darts out and bangs the door after her.*)

People's laughter would smother me.

(FANNY *goes slowly up towards the fire.*)

CURTAIN

SCENE IV

Same scene: later the same evening. Kitchen empty; lamp burning; door shut. The door opens and JOHNNY *and* CORNEY *in oilskins oxter* PADDY *between them.* JOHNNY *shuts the door.*

PADDY Wasn't it duncey it happened me? My head just went spinning and spinning, and the next thing I knew was Dan wetting my lips with whisky. But I'm alright: it's nonsense them making me stay ashore.

CORNEY It's no nonsense.

JOHNNY It's it that's no nonsense; for one night.

PADDY God send Kitty doesn't hear it or she'll put me home to bed: I'm alright. Look-at, there's the makings of punch for us all in this. (*He takes*

63

a bottle out of his pocket) Johnny, you're the boy to make the punch. It's the kind of a night that a sup of punch is good for everybody. (*Goes to the fire and shakes the kettle to discover whether there's water in it and then hangs it into the blaze*)

CORNEY (*following Paddy up the floor*) To tell you the truth it's not any too friendly a night at all; maybe, it is that I have a touch of a cold, there's a tightness in my breathing, somehow.

PADDY You can't beat a sup of punch for any tightness in your breathing. And this is no night for Johnny to go out with them legs of his without something in him to keep them warm.

JOHNNY Well, indeed, it might do them same legs no harm, as you say. (*He rests the bottle on the dresser, picks up a jug and looks into it*)

CORNEY Since we got ready and sat waiting for the tide to take us down the Narrows, I'm less and less struck on that night: I said it to you, Johnny:

I didn't like that dawn this morning: and I didn't like that sun this evening: and I have my own suspicion of the moon out there: it'll be a night's slaving with the sea, mark my words.

JOHNNY You've a touch of cold, Corney, and it's in your bones. Peter Dan is venturesome and very venturesome, but you can trust a night that he'll trust. I have that steadied now these years. I'd as soon watch Peter Dan's movements as watch the sky any day; I have him that well steadied. (*Gathers up three glasses, jug and bottle*)

PADDY What put it into his head to go out at all the night?

CORNEY It's equal to us what put it into his head. Could you hold back them boys of ours now? Could you hold back the tide?

JOHNNY (*approaching the table*) And would you blame them? I be steadying the young people too. They don't thole things the way we used to thole them. But maybe, that's what's wrong with us, we thole too much. Give them their heads. The young people is alright.

CORNEY I have a houseful up there and I'm willing to give them all the head they want. Where have they to turn? They turn on one another betimes; sure enough, it would be wrong to keep them ashore if there was anything to be got out in the Bay.

JOHNNY If Peter Dan thinks there is fish in the Bay I'll back Peter Dan. But I wouldn't say they'll be there long. Where's them herrin' I had in my sou'wester? (*Picks up sou'wester from chair and empties a few herring on to a plate, goes closer to* PADDY *and* CORNEY *with the plate in his hand*) Now, look here, do you see anything strange in that class of herrin' Corney? Or you Paddy?

CORNEY I wish, Johnny, you'd keep your talk away from wonders that nobody can see but yourself. What's strange about them herrin' more then any other herrin' of the same quality?

JOHNNY Then why don't they behave the way herrin' did long ago? Who'll answer me that? I may be wrong, but it's my opinion them's a tramp class of herrin'; they put me in mind of tinkers at a fair. They are a healthy enough fish. They have a fine colour. There's a good, rich, solid flesh on them. But they're a tramp class of herrin'; they won't rest long anywhere, mark my words.

CORNEY There's talk for an island man. Peter Dan sees the weather might snap again, and he is venturing one rush out when he thinks he saw some signs of fish. Johnny is getting worse, Paddy; between the youngsters finding fault with everything and Johnny making a wonder of everything, we are to be pitied.

PADDY I'm to be pitied to be in and you all going out. What spinning came on my head at all? (*The kettle boils and he takes it over and hands it to* JOHNNY)

PADDY We'll use a grain of my sugar; my boys can easy enough get some at the boathouse in the morning, if they're lucky enough to have business to the Port at all. (*Fishes out sugar in paper from his pocket*)

JOHNNY (*making the punch in the jug*) Corney thinks me strange, Paddy, because I be steadying on things. Maybe, Corney is right about Peter Dan wanting to run out and back before the weather can stop him. And, maybe, again Peter Dan knows that that breed of herrin' could show their nose one day and be gone the next. Peter Dan knows the class of fish them is, and he's afraid they might be passed without him having a drag out of them.

PADDY Peter Dan would know whatever there is to know, and he was out in the bay this evening himself.

CORNEY And weren't we all out in the bay? Maybe, Peter Dan was talking to the herrin'; maybe, Johnny will be telling us next that herrin' can talk. That's how Johnny makes Peter Dan out to be queer, he thinks queer things about him; it's easy to make men out to be queer that way.

JOHNNY And that's just a thing I do be steadying on too, Paddy Cormac; why shouldn't herrin' talk? I don't mean talk like Christians, God forbid; it would be the last thing I'd do to compare the dumb animal to a human being: but hasn't every animal a noise of its own? The very cricket makes a noise of its own. I'm not as dark to things as Corney, and I'm often thinking that some smart man somewhere will find a way to listen to herrin'. Man alive, millions of them guttering water in their gills itself, isn't that a sound that could be heard? Some smart man will find out some way to hear it some day, but it won't be Corney.

CORNEY Honest to God, Paddy, if I didn't know the breed of Johnny through and through I'd be worried about Johnny.

JOHNNY Corney never will allow, Paddy Cormac, that there's sense in anything I say. I be mad betimes. You wouldn't think it now but I do.

CORNEY Well, under heavens, what does Johnny

want me to give into Paddy Cormac? To give in
that animals makes a noise: that dogs bark, that
cats meow, that crickets cricket? Look-at, my
head is getting light. Leave me be. I'll get no
good of my punch if my mind is not let settle.

JOHNNY Leave Corney be, Paddy Cormac; leave
Corney be, leave Corney to God. Well, good luck
to us all, Corney and all. (*Picks up two glasses and
holds them out to* PADDY *and* CORNEY)

(*The door comes in and* HUGHIE BOYLE *appears
in the doorway,* BRIGID *behind him.*)

HUGHIE Well, you three old rogues; now, don't
spend the night over it.

JOHNNY (*hastily withdraws glasses and empties
them back into the jug*) You're just in time, Hughie;
just in time; and Brigid, you'll have a taste too;
we'll all have a taste.

(*Hurries to the dresser, can find only one
extra glass; takes that and a cup, hurries back*

to table to make five shares of punch. BRIGID *and* HUGHIE *come inside.* BRIGID *shuts the door after her.*)

CORNEY I get no good of my punch unless I'm pleased with the whole world. Johnny has my mind near capsized. Hughie, a mhic, you'll sing me yon song. You promised me you'd get the words from the 'Highland Mary'. A song's a grand thing to get into your head with punch. (JOHNNY *is carefully measuring out the punch again*)

HUGHIE But, damn it, Corney, we must be off.

CORNEY One verse itself: ask him you, Brigid: look-at, it would make a new man of me.

(BRIGID *and* HUGHIE *look at each other and smile.*)

CORNEY That's a boy, Hughie.

(CORNEY *begins to hum 'The Road to the Isles'.*

71

HUGHIE *breaks in with the words.* CORNEY *becomes silent. His face lights up: he beats time with his free hand.* JOHNNY *silently hands each his glass and keeps the cup himself.* BRIGID *joins in for a few bars and then goes silent suddenly, and sits down. Towards the end of the second chorus* HUGHIE *jerks her to her feet: she joins in obviously with an effort. He repeats the chorus: he sings with spirit:* BRIGID *responds to the challenge.* CORNEY *goes on beating time to himself after the song has died down.* BRIGID *and* HUGHIE *look amused at* CORNEY.)

JOHNNY (*to* PADDY) Corney's a strange man. Man alive, wouldn't I be the happy man if I could get Corney to put the same heed in my talk as he puts in them songs. And if they were songs with meaning in them itself, like 'Donnelly and Cooper,' or 'My Name's Pat O'Donnell,' I could see into it. (*Picks up his oil-coat*) Now, not a thing at all could I make out of that song of Hughie's. Could you, Paddy Cormac?

72

PADDY Well, now that you say it, Johnny, not a bit of sense was in it. What was it about anyway? I'll go to the shore with you.

HUGHIE Out with us.

(HUGHIE *gives* CORNEY *a poke in the ribs: picks up oilskins and goes to the door. He sprinkles the men with holy water as they pass out. He raises his fingers to sprinkle back at* BRIGID, *catches look of gloom on her face and pauses. She brightens quickly. He sprinkles the holy water and goes out.* BRIGID *drops her attempt at brightness and comes slowly down the floor.* FANNY BRIAN *comes in, comes quickly up to* BRIGID *and faces her.* BRIGID *steps aside and goes towards the open door and leans against the door post looking out.* FANNY *goes to the fire and stands looking into the blaze.*)

CURTAIN

SCENE V

*Johnny Anthon's boat in the bay. The glow of the
lanthorn, which* JOHNNY *has between his legs to keep them
warm, is on his face. Three other dark sou'westered
figures are in the boat. There is the ripple of water
against the sides of the boat. A voice drones two lines
of a Come-all-ye:*

> *'With haughty pride he said abide,*
> *In Fanad by the sea*
> *For you'll never wed the daughter of*
> *Mael Morra an Bhata Bhuidhe.'*

VOICE IN BOAT Look out, here's somebody.
(JOHNNY *lanthorn in hand jumps up, holds lanthorn
aloft*)

HUGHIE (*in the dark, a little distant*) Is that you,
Johnny Anthon?

JOHNNY It's me, Hughie Boyle.

75

WRACK

HUGHIE You had no luck more than ourselves.

JOHNNY Not a bit of luck, Hughie, this is our fourth shot.

HUGHIE We're going out on the Lenane for a quick, last venture. There's fish around. Boats went home hours ago with good catches.

JOHNNY I know; Paddy Cormac's boys passed myself. Paddy's boys'll have the laugh at Paddy. What do you think of the night?

HUGHIE The sea is getting lumpy: the night won't last. We'll just shoot and haul.

JOHNNY It wouldn't be my judgement either to depend too much on this night. But Peter Dan's the judge. Do you think it's worth while hanging on, Peter Dan?

PETER DAN (*strong voice in the distance*) There's a strong fresh smell of fish in the wind here, but if the fouls catch us, mind, it's a question of cutting away from any nets still out. This water is a broth of fouls. If one bursts they all burst. (*Sounds of oars as Peter Dan's boat passes*)

JOHNNY (*sniffing audibly*) I had the notion, mind you, that there is a strong smell of fish here. Well, maybe in God. (JOHNNY *gets slowly back to his seat*)

A VOICE If God doesn't save us some boat'll cut us down . . . queer place to keep the lanthorn.

JOHNNY Well, now, little as it is, the heat of the lanthorn keeps my legs in humour. I'll put it up when we go to travel. Nobody is going to travel without light, so we're safe enough. (*Silence. A voice in boat drones two lines of 'Highland Mary'*)

JOHNNY (*breaking in on song*) I should have asked Peter Dan if he saw Corney: it's a wonder none of you thought of asking if he saw Corney.

A VOICE What the devil would he know about Corney?

WRACK

JOHNNY I'm never at my ease in this bit of water. We're the farthest into the fouls except Peter Dan. The sea hatches all its tantrums in a place like this.

A VOICE (*sharply*) Bedamn, there goes somebody after Peter Dan . . . over there to windward. I'll swear that's Corney.

JOHNNY Call to him one of you; call to Corney.

A VOICE Call into that distance, and the smashing of the sea around his boat, and, anyway, Corney is no mainland man. The sea is open to him.

JOHNNY Them sons of Corney's are venturesome and headstrong. They'd dare anything for a catch of fish. Try will he hear you.

A VOICE (*impatiently*) What roaring would we be at? And, by heavens, if I thought there was herrin' there we would be off too.

JOHNNY YOU heard Peter Dan yourself as well as me . . . by the time we could haul now. . . .

WRACK

A VOICE But he went out himself, didn't he? I'm
sick and tired hearing about Peter Dan.

JOHNNY That's no talk at all, so it's not. There's
no real meaning in that talk. Every tail that is got
this night is got through Peter Dan.

A VOICE A fat lot of good that is to us. Why
don't we haul, and if we have nothing got, can't
we go in there after Peter Dan and Corney? (*A
short pause*)

JOHNNY Every chance yon was Corney you saw, I
suppose . . . Them's good boys of Corney's. I
wish they wouldn't let the world put their tempers
up. A fisherman must watch that. That's how the
sea breaks many a man: puts his temper up first.
Bad times and broken weather, many a temper that
breaks: I have that steadied.

A VOICE Well, wouldn't it madden anybody . . .
the fish is there for other boats got them . . . this is
our fourth shot for nothing. Wouldn't the like of

that madden any man. I'll swear to you Peter Dan is just dashing round in a rage himself.

JOHNNY Peter Dan's different: but, mind what I'm saying to you the longest day you live, never let the sea rise you, for if you do it has you bate. I have that steadied.

SINGER Seo me láimh duit nach bhfuil me pósta gur buachaill óg me, a thug gean do mhnaoi.

VOICE I wish to God you'd learn a song through and through or else shut your mouth. One thing I can't stand is a verse of this and a verse of that and the end of nothing. (*A sharp whistle in the distance*)

JOHNNY That's Hughie Boyle. He's calling Corney: listen . . . (*A short pause*) That's the way he calls Corney or me and us in the bog. All Ellen ever does is shake on Hughie and Hughie whistles. Listen . . .

VOICE You'd think Corney was daft the way you're clucking about him. Corney is in a boat on the sea like the rest of us, isn't he?

JOHNNY Whist, can't you. (*The whistle comes again.* JOHNNY *gets to his feet*) Come on my boys, we'll haul. If Peter Dan is that restless, let us all get out of here. Corney will come for that too. Corney will put heed in a call from Peter Dan's boat. Come on, haul.

(JOHNNY *moves to the stern of the boat; the other men come forward to haul nets.*)

VOICE If we have nothing this time we'll go farther out, we will, if the whole Atlantic was in suds; I won't go home empty-handed out of this sea this night.

JOHNNY Other people, maybe, is as much pushed as you; that's not the talk of a fisherman. Go on, haul.

WRACK

(Sounds of oars being pushed aside, rasp of cable against gunwale, sharper ripple of water.)

CREW *(excited shout)* HERRIN'.

VOICE By heavens, we have them. Ho-ho, me whistlers! Three cheers for old Ireland.

(Rasp of rope, grunts—waves splashing against bows. In the distance boom of a bursting foul. Distant shout.)

JOHNNY Stop! Is that a shout I hear. STOP. A minute CAN'T YOU. I'd swear I heard . . . Where in the world is Corney? That sea is not at all to my liking . . . *(Calls)* CORNEY.

VOICE What heed would you put in a shout — while we're gaping around in the dark the dog fish will be tearing our nets and spoiling the fish.

JOHNNY Always put heed in what might be the shout of a neighbour wanting you.

WRACK

(Shoal water bursts near at hand. Sudden rise of wind.)

CREW FOUL.

(Hauling feverishly renewed.)

JOHNNY It's a hard word to say, but it's a word must be said: come on, now, it's murder, but we must do it — out with your knives. What is in the water must stay there. OUT with your knives.

VOICE We have fish and we'll take them in or sink.

(Grunts of approval, feverish hauling.)

JOHNNY But, good God, man, you heard Peter Dan . . .

VOICE To hell with Peter Dan.

JOHNNY *(after a pause)* Well, I'm no coward

more than the rest of you, but I'm in charge here no longer. Come on this helm you, Dan. (*Moves forward in the boat*)

voice It's alright, father, we have them nearly in. A Chríosta!

(*Water breaks at the bows of the boat and boils down on them in the green darkness.*)

johnny Grab a taft. HOLD ON. GRAB.

(*Water sweeping the boat puts out the lanthorn. Noise of storm. No talk from crew for a moment.*)

We're afloat! WE'RE AFLOAT. Leave the bailing to me, leave the cutting to Dan. ON YOUR OARS. I was through the like of this. . .

CURTAIN

SCENE VI

(*Hughie Boyle's kitchen near dawn. Storm raging outside. Kitchen in darkness. Door opens, two figures enter, and close the door behind them.*)

MAN'S VOICE Do you think she could be asleep through all that?

WOMAN'S VOICE I doubt it, I doubt it.

> (*Man strikes match and shows* PADDY CORMAC *and* KITTY. *He lights lamp.*)

KITTY (*going to the hearth*) This fire was never raked. God help her, she's out in all that, and no knowing where to look for her. All we can do is build a fire. She'll be a block of ice. Bring me up turf. (KITTY *lifts out coals,* PADDY *takes armful of turf from box at the foot of the table*) There's no

85

knowing what story the morning will have to tell. Thank God for the good luck our boys had to get their catch early. Yon sea is not human.

PADDY (*leaving turf on hearth*) It must be near the dawn now; a storm eases with the light. (*He gets down on one knee and helps to build the fire*)

KITTY The light will be slow in coming for the sky is full of blackness, and the storm is thick with the sea. Man or mortal never saw the sea in such a rage. (*Turns to put water into the kettle from a pail near the dresser*) Where, under God, is poor Brigid? (*Approaches fire with kettle*) Get down on your knees, Paddy and blow the fire.

> (*She hangs on the kettle. A gust of wind sweeps through the house.* BRIGID *enters, shuts the door by pressing her back against it and stands there.* KITTY *rushes to her, puts the latch on the door, takes* BRIGID's *hands in hers.*)

You're frozen stiff. Amn't a glad the fire is kindled. Come over to the fire, Brigid, like a good girl.

(BRIGID *allows herself to be taken across the floor*) I'll make a hot drink for us all. The kettle is near boiling.

PADDY The morning will soon be here now. A storm eases with the light.

(KITTY *fusses round the fire.*)

BRIGID Morning is here. And, oh God, yon waves!

PADDY They saw it coming and ran for shelter. That's what they done Brigid.

BRIGID There was no time to run anywhere. I was sitting there. The door came in. I got a start; often it came in this week if the latch is not put on right and I got no start. I said I was foolish. I shut the door. I sat here swithering would I go to bed, or go out to look at the night. In the end I went out. The sky was tight, with darkness coming into it like bruises. I came in. I tried to quieten myself. I couldn't rest. I shook the holy water. And I done a thing I never done in my life before, I called

87

Hughie. I called him out loud. 'HUGHIE,' I said, 'HEAD FOR HOME.' I prayed the Mother of God to head him for home. I came back in. I sat there in the corner. Everything was terrible quiet. I mind how the dry crinkling of the burning coals grew loud in my ears; it kind of smothered me. I got frightened. I dashed out. The sky was in ribbons. Black blasts were sousing themselves against the rocks. The world was shaking, and the sea, the sea — it was up in the sky and it roaring. I think I fell, maybe a blast tossed me.

KITTY Here, my girl, stop your nonsense, and drink this; you're foundered. (*Holds out bowl of tea.* BRIGID *takes it and sips listlessly*) And, now Paddy, it will ease all our hearts to pray. Put a head on the rosary; just get down on your knees here, Brigid, before the fire and pray in your mind as you drink your tea.

BRIGID (*placing the bowl suddenly in* KITTY's *hands*) I can't pray. If I pray I'll screech. If I open my mouth to pray I'll SCREECH.

KITTY (*leaves bowl out of her hand on table*) You'll shut your mouth till you see if you have cause to screech. The morning will soon be here; the morning will bring news to put the heart singing in you.

(*Blast shakes the house.*)

BRIGID Hughie is out in that. What headway can talk make when Hughie is out in that.

(*Walks down the floor.* KITTY *and* PADDY *look at each other helplessly.* KITTY *follows* BRIGID.)

KITTY (*jerking* BRIGID *round to face her*) Ah, shut your mouth, Brigid Hughie. Isn't it Peter Dan's boat you're talking about — the greatest crew ever was on this island, and this islandmen the best boatsmen in the world. What could a storm do to a boat like that? Think of that, Brigid; wasn't it knowing the way Paddy was such a good helmsman used to keep the heart in me.

BRIGID Ah! Kitty, Kitty — us women, we're all

alike. All night I'm living on words like that. (*Roar of the storm swells out*) Ah, Virgin Mother this night, what shelter are words for my heart against that? The sea has the world down and it will murder every living thing it can reach.

KITTY God is stronger than the storm, Brigid, God is stronger than the storm.

BRIGID Hughie got trapped. It was Hughie the storm trapped; me over there all night on the rocks; boats wrung in out of the darkness one by one, and no Hughie. If I could only leap out into the heart of that darkness and land in the boat with Hughie . . . and then the light came and I saw the waves. I'll never be able to look on the sea again. But what brought me in? I must be out waiting for Hughie; no matter how the sea gives him to me I'll be waiting. I must be waiting.

(*She dashes to the door.* KITTY *wrestles with her and drags her back.*)

KITTY Listen to me, Brigid, I'm ashamed of you.

You're making no fight; Peter Dan's crew battering their way through the sea, it's on your knees you should be. It's God alone can help them now. What help can you give except to ask God to help them — it will ease your heart too.

BRIGID There's one fear on me all the time, that they went to help somebody. But, surely, surely, if they went to help somebody God would help them. Amn't I the bad woman to miss a minute without praying?

(*She drops on her knees.* PADDY *is fishing out his beads. Door is flung open and* FANNY BRIAN *enters, hair in disorder, clothes wet and mud-stained, blood on one arm.* KITTY *shuts the door.* FANNY *raises the caoineadh. It snaps and she breaks into words.*)

FANNY BRIAN Donough's boat is in. Anthon's boat is in. They are all in. It's as I saw it. The sea has its play over now. Charlie's lost. Our men is lost, Brigid Hughie.

91

BRIGID If any boat that was caught out on the fishing grounds lived to come in now Hughie'll come. If any crew blasts a way home now, Peter Dan's boat'll come. Fanny Brian, I tell you, they'll come. (*Her passion dies suddenly and she moans*) Peter Dan's boat couldn't be the one not to come in. God wouldn't do that and the sea couldn't.

FANNY The thick thighs of the waves crushed the life out of our men, for I saw it. I saw the sea, smooth like a child's skin, with the fouls in a tremble to leap through and smash the whole world around them. I saw the storm that was putting the fouls mad stealing up behind the darkness bent for a spring; and the boats going out, and the sea silent, making play with them.

BRIGID And when the fouls leaped, would Hughie be asleep? Would Peter Dan be shiftless? Wouldn't their oars skiver the thick thighs of the fouls to get to where the sea is human.

FANNY I saw the wee timber boats going out into

the darkness. I heard the roar of the fouls and the bursting of blasts, and before my very eyes the wee timber boats went whirling round. And then I saw a big coffin drifting helpless in the sea, and a sail peeling itself off a mast and winding itself round the bodies of dead men. It was Peter Dan's boat.

BRIGID A coffin? I painted the gunwale on Peter Dan's boat — a coffin? I fixed the holy water bottle in the bows — a coffin. Hughie knew. That's what put boat-building in Hughie's mind. Hughie knew. HUGHIE, why didn't you tell me? Why didn't God let me see? I would have told everybody, everybody. Why didn't somebody see it and tell us all? Only us all to see it wouldn't we tumble the world to get peace and a footing for the poor. Hughie . . . (*sinks on to a chair*)

(*There is hammering at the door.* PADDY CORMAC *opens it. Oilskinned men pile in.* JOHNNY ANTHON, *exhausted, is pushed to the front.* BRIGID *starts to her feet, facing them,*

93

searching. JOHNNY *takes off his sou'wester. He is dazed, scarcely aware of his surroundings.*)

JOHNNY Could it naturally be that we all came in and that Peter Dan and Corney could be lost?

PADDY Lost, Johnny, lost?

JOHNNY We were caught tethered into the fouls by a net; I'm steadying, maybe, it was that saved us. It came sudden and no boat deep in yonder could naturally live. But, could Peter Dan drown? Could Corney?

(FANNY BRIAN *comes down the floor;* JOHNNY'S *eyes are drawn to her. He shuffles a step forward.*)

FANNY Tell me this, Corney called?

JOHNNY I can't get it out of my mind but it was Corney's call I heard. God help me, Paddy, if Corney called and me not to go to Corney.

FANNY   Corney called. My curse on you for breakers that didn't smother Corney before he could call. Corney called, and nobody but Peter Dan heard Corney. My curse on you for a night. My curse on you for an island. My thousand curses on the hungry belly of the sea.

KITTY   In God's Name get you on your knees all of you.

(Drops on her knees. BRIGID *dashes to the door and pulls it open; a gust of wind puts out the lamp. There is a struggle around the door.* KITTY's *voice alone sounds in the rosary in the darkness.)*

CURTAIN

Date Due

PR6029   .D55W7
O'Donnell, Peadar
Wrack

DATE	ISSUED TO
	91061

91061

Lightning Source UK Ltd.
Milton Keynes UK
UKHW021940090223
416794UK00012B/134